This Is America

The American Spirit in Places and People

Don Robb

Illustrated by Christine Joy Pratt

ini Charlesbridge

To my friend
Julie
who has more
spirit than
most!
Don Robb
2008

To Will, who is full of spirit, from Poppy
—D. R.

In gratitude to the first Americans in my family,
brave pilgrims and Italian immigrants, and for
Owen Thomas Burke, our newest American
—C. J. P.

Published by Charlesbridge
85 Main Street
Watertown, MA 02472
(617) 926-0329
www.charlesbridge.com

Library of Congress Cataloging-in-Publication Data
Robb, Don.
This is America : the American spirit in places and people / Donald Robb.
    p. cm.
    ISBN 1-57091-604-7 (reinforced for library use)
    ISBN 1-57091-605-5 (softcover)
1. United States—Civilization—Juvenile literature. 2. Historic sites—United States—Juvenile literature.
3. Civil rights—United States—Juvenile literature. I. Pratt, Christine Joy, ill. II. Title.
E169.1.R72135 2005
973—dc22   2004003308

Printed in Korea
(hc) 10 9 8 7 6 5 4 3 2 1
(sc) 10 9 8 7 6 5 4 3 2 1

Illustrations done in scratchboard and watercolor
Display type set in Mayflower by P22 and text type set in Adobe Caslon
Color separated, printed, and bound by Sung In Printing, Korea
Production supervision by Brian G. Walker
Designed by Susan Mallory Sherman

What is America?

It's a land of great beauty, stretching from ocean to ocean. It's many different people, with roots all over the world. And most of all, it's the ideals we all believe in and the dreams we all share.

We call those ideals and dreams the American spirit—the spirit that holds us together as a nation. It's what America is all about.

At different times and in different places, this spirit has been tested and challenged. In this book, you'll visit places where the American spirit has met these challenges. You'll discover that spirit in the words and actions of some famous Americans.

These places and these people show us how the experiences of the past have shaped the spirit that links us together as Americans today.

Liberty

To Americans, liberty means the right to choose our own leaders, to work and live and worship where we please, to enjoy the rights our Constitution gives us, and to follow our dreams wherever they lead us.

Concord Bridge

American liberty was born early one spring morning in 1775. American colonists were angry that the British king had taken away rights that they felt belonged to them. When King George sent British troops out from Boston, a group of farmers met them at a wooden bridge over the Concord River. They wanted to force the British back to Boston. None of them knew that the shots they fired that day would start America's war for independence.

Dixville Notch

The right to vote is an important liberty that Americans share. We vote for local and state leaders and members of Congress. Every four years, we elect the president of the United States. In the tiny town of Dixville Notch, New Hampshire, voters still go to the polls at midnight on Election Day to cast their ballots. They are the first Americans each election to exercise this important right.

USS *Constitution*

One of the freedoms Americans enjoy is the right to sail the seas. In the early years of our nation, the crew of the *Constitution* bravely guarded American ships against pirate attacks in the Caribbean and Mediterranean seas. During a second war with Britain in 1812, the ship helped Americans keep our freedom and never lost a battle. The *Constitution* is now docked in Boston, Massachusetts.

Thomas Jefferson

Most of the words in the Declaration of Independence came from Thomas Jefferson. He believed very strongly in the rights of all people. Liberty, to him, meant the right to make decisions without the government telling people what to do or to think. In the Declaration Jefferson spelled out what rights he believed all Americans should share: "life, liberty, and the pursuit of happiness."

Equality

Without equality, liberty is a hollow dream. Until all people are equal, no one can fully enjoy the blessings of liberty. Throughout the years Americans of all kinds have fought for equality.

Levi Coffin House

For African American slaves, equality was almost impossible to imagine. Yet thousands of slaves, inspired by brave leaders like Harriet Tubman and Frederick Douglass, escaped from plantations in the South. They followed secret routes, called the "Underground Railroad," to Canada. The home of Levi and Catharine Coffin in Indiana was one of many safe stopping places along the way. More than 2,000 slaves found shelter here on their way to freedom and equality.

Wesleyan Chapel

Women, too, had to struggle to gain equality. Meeting in the Wesleyan Chapel in Seneca Falls, New York, some 250 women and 40 men drafted the Declaration of Sentiments in 1848. Written by Elizabeth Cady Stanton, this document said that "all men and women are created equal." It demanded that women be given the right to vote, to own property, and to enjoy other rights that men had. Only part of the original chapel stands today, but the dream of equal rights lives on.

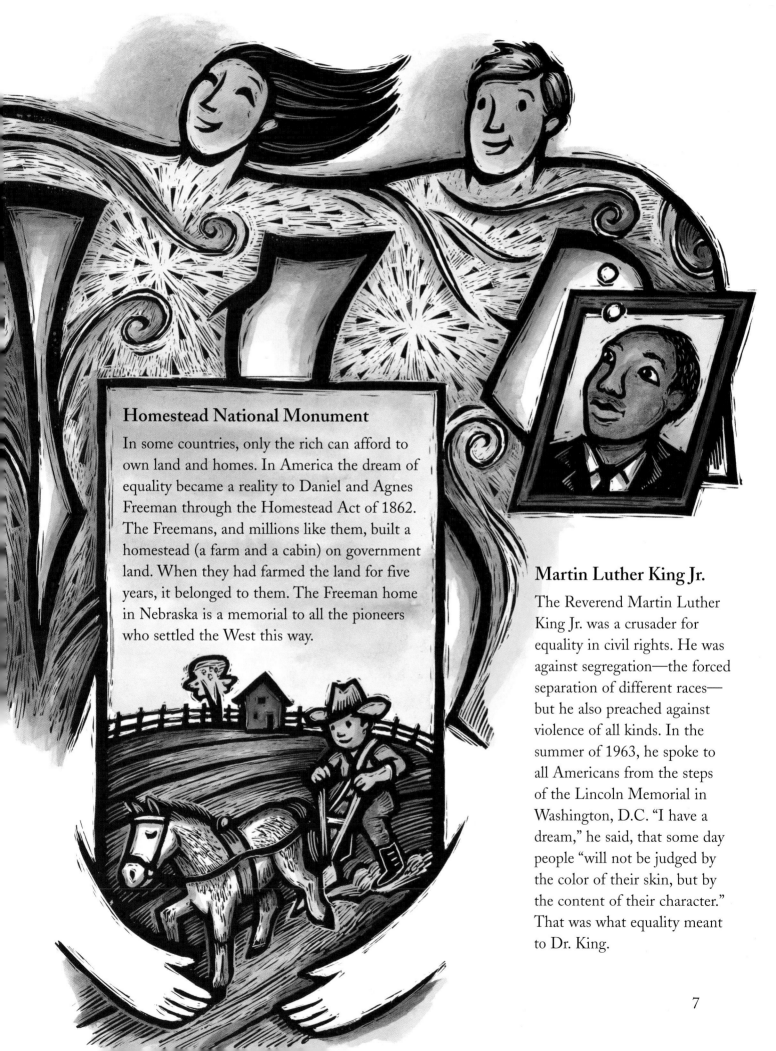

Homestead National Monument

In some countries, only the rich can afford to own land and homes. In America the dream of equality became a reality to Daniel and Agnes Freeman through the Homestead Act of 1862. The Freemans, and millions like them, built a homestead (a farm and a cabin) on government land. When they had farmed the land for five years, it belonged to them. The Freeman home in Nebraska is a memorial to all the pioneers who settled the West this way.

Martin Luther King Jr.

The Reverend Martin Luther King Jr. was a crusader for equality in civil rights. He was against segregation—the forced separation of different races—but he also preached against violence of all kinds. In the summer of 1963, he spoke to all Americans from the steps of the Lincoln Memorial in Washington, D.C. "I have a dream," he said, that some day people "will not be judged by the color of their skin, but by the content of their character." That was what equality meant to Dr. King.

Legal Rights

If people are truly equal, they must all have the same rights. A right is an important privilege written into our laws to protect our basic liberties. These rights help make us, and keep us, a free people.

Independence Hall

All of the basic ideals of liberty that we Americans believe in can be found in our Declaration of Independence and our Constitution. The Declaration lists the rights and liberties the colonists felt the British had denied them. The Constitution sets up a system of government that protects these rights. Both documents were signed in Independence Hall in Philadelphia, Pennsylvania.

Federal Hall Memorial

One part of our Constitution, called the Bill of Rights, lists the special rights that every American is entitled to. They include the right to say what we think (freedom of speech), worship as we please (freedom of religion), publish what we wish (freedom of the press), and gather peacefully together (freedom of assembly). The old Federal Hall in New York City, where the Bill of Rights was written, has been torn down, but the Federal Hall Memorial is a reminder of the importance of our individual rights.

Plymouth Rock

On a November day in 1620, a brave group of 88 settlers from England aboard the *Mayflower* landed near Plymouth, Massachusetts. They came because they did not approve of the rules of the Church of England. These Pilgrims, as they came to be called, were the first to come to America so they could enjoy the right to worship as they pleased. Today, this right is so important to us that it is protected in our Constitution.

Cesar Chavez

American workers have fought long and hard for the right to join unions so that they can work together for higher pay, health care, safe working conditions, and pensions. Cesar Chavez, a farm worker in California, led the effort in the 1960s to organize some of America's poorest laborers. He convinced millions of Americans not to buy California grapes until growers agreed to increase wages and provide other benefits to their workers. Like Martin Luther King Jr., Chavez believed in nonviolence as a way to win important rights.

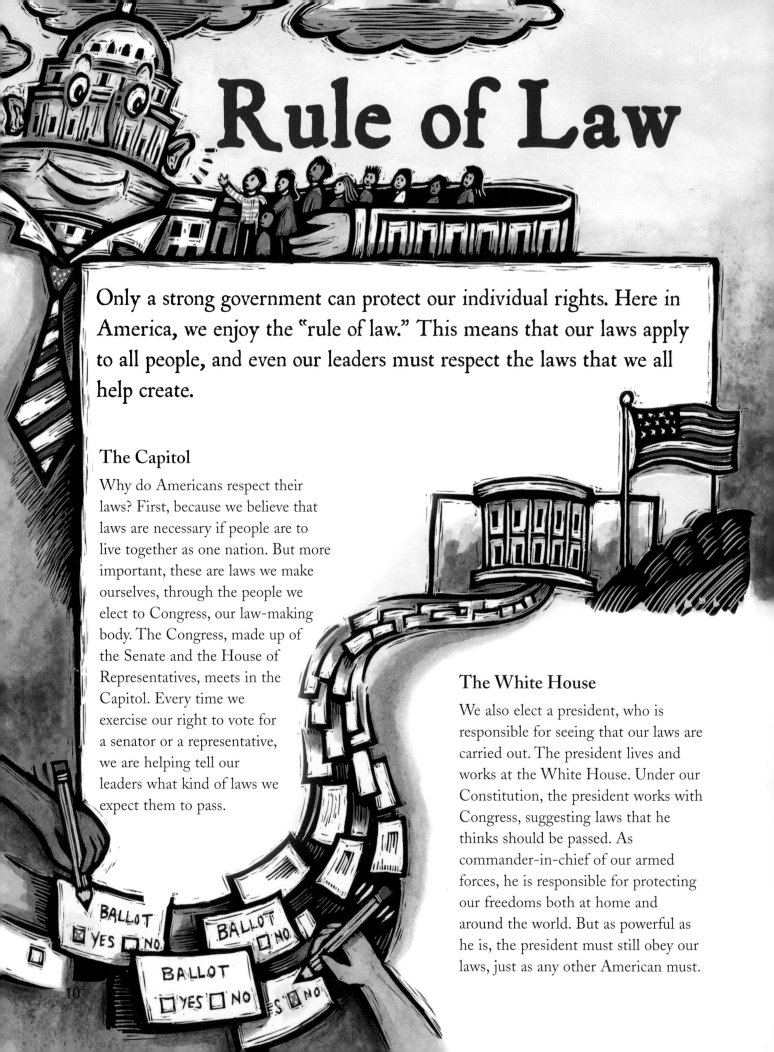

Rule of Law

Only a strong government can protect our individual rights. Here in America, we enjoy the "rule of law." This means that our laws apply to all people, and even our leaders must respect the laws that we all help create.

The Capitol

Why do Americans respect their laws? First, because we believe that laws are necessary if people are to live together as one nation. But more important, these are laws we make ourselves, through the people we elect to Congress, our law-making body. The Congress, made up of the Senate and the House of Representatives, meets in the Capitol. Every time we exercise our right to vote for a senator or a representative, we are helping tell our leaders what kind of laws we expect them to pass.

The White House

We also elect a president, who is responsible for seeing that our laws are carried out. The president lives and works at the White House. Under our Constitution, the president works with Congress, suggesting laws that he thinks should be passed. As commander-in-chief of our armed forces, he is responsible for protecting our freedoms both at home and around the world. But as powerful as he is, the president must still obey our laws, just as any other American must.

The Supreme Court

The document that created our form of government is our Constitution. The job of the Supreme Court is to interpret, or explain, what the Constitution means. Sometimes people object to a law that has been passed. Then the Supreme Court decides if Congress followed all the many rules of the Constitution when it passed the law. These rules help protect the freedoms and rights of all Americans. If Congress has not followed all the rules, the Supreme Court can declare the law "unconstitutional," and it is no longer a law.

Thurgood Marshall

As a young lawyer, Thurgood Marshall specialized in cases dealing with civil rights—cases where he believed the law was not being applied fairly to all people. His most important case, *Brown v. Board of Education*, came in 1954. He convinced the Supreme Court that sending children to different schools on the basis of their race was wrong. The Court ordered state leaders to end segregated schools and treat all students equally. A few years later, Marshall himself was appointed to the Supreme Court, where he served for 24 years.

Pioneer Spirit

Pioneers are people who try out new ideas and new forms of government. Pioneers are not afraid to explore new places or to follow their dreams to new frontiers. American pioneers changed the face of a whole continent, and even today are seeking new challenges.

Acoma Pueblo

More than 10,000 years ago, the very first American pioneers arrived in North America from Asia. They explored and settled the whole continent, hunting, fishing, planting, and building cities. These Native Americans turned a wilderness into a home for themselves and millions of others who would later come to America. Acoma Pueblo in New Mexico is one of the earliest Native American settlements and is the oldest continually occupied home site in America.

Scotts Bluff

Millions of men, women, and children followed their dreams along the dusty trails across the Great Plains to Oregon and California in the late 1800s. Along the way they faced biting cold and scorching heat, thirst and starvation, as well as the constant threat of attack by Native Americans defending their homelands. The ruts of their wagon wheels still mark the Nebraska countryside around Scotts Bluff. Here weary travelers found a day or two of rest and supplies of fresh water and firewood before they set out again.

Kennedy Space Center

Space is the frontier for modern pioneers. The Kennedy Space Center at Cape Canaveral, Florida, is the home of America's space program, where scientists and astronauts work together. From Cape Canaveral, the first American astronauts were sent to the moon. Space Center scientists launch rocket ships to probe the planets and shuttles to carry astronauts and equipment between Earth and the international space station. Here the pioneer dream lives on.

Sacagawea

Guiding Meriwether Lewis and William Clark as they explored America's new western lands in the early 1800s was a young Shoshone woman, Sacagawea. Sacagawea was invaluable to the expedition. Her knowledge of the western river valleys and mountain passes guided this pioneering expedition along its way. Fluent in several Native American languages, she could communicate with the people whose lands the explorers passed through and bargain with them for necessities such as food, lodging, and supplies.

Hardship

Americans understand that liberty and freedom can come at a high cost. The men and women who built this country often endured hardships. And there have been times when we Americans have forgotten our ideals of liberty and equality and have caused hardships to others.

Jamestown

A small band of English settlers landed in America in May 1607 after a rough four-month sea journey. Food was scarce, and many of the colonists died of disease in the strange new land. Life was so hard that during the winter of 1609–1610—called the "starving time"—most of the original settlers died. But a few survived. More women and children followed them. Soon the little settlement of Jamestown became the center of a thriving Virginia colony.

Valley Forge

It was December 1777. General George Washington and his men took refuge in drafty log huts near Valley Forge for the winter. The British settled into comfortable homes 18 miles away in Philadelphia. They kept warm; they ate well. Washington's troops lived on meager rations and often went hungry. They lacked warm clothing and blankets. Many were barefoot; all suffered from the cold. Yet every day they drilled to keep their spirits up. By spring they were ready again to take up the fight for independence.

Manzanar

Japanese Americans faced special hardships during World War II, after Japanese planes bombed Pearl Harbor. Many people in this country felt threatened by anyone of Japanese ancestry. As a result thousands of loyal, innocent Japanese Americans were forcibly removed from their homes, their farms, and their businesses. They spent the war years living in miserable conditions in temporary camps such as Manzanar in California. Because of wartime paranoia, these Americans were forced to give up their freedoms. In 1988 the U.S. government finally publicly apologized for its treatment of Japanese Americans during the war.

Clara Barton

Americans have tried whenever possible to ease the hardships of others and comfort those who suffer. During the Civil War, wounded soldiers suffered horribly. Clara Barton was one of many volunteers who tended to the wounded brought in from the front lines. Barton was so persistent that she was allowed to go directly to the front, where she could provide immediate aid. After the war she founded the American Red Cross, which helps relieve hardship in times of war or disaster.

Courage

America is a nation built on the courage of its people. Courage is that spirit inside each of us that makes it possible to do our duty whatever the cost: to face dangers, overcome hardship, fight for our dreams, and reach our goals.

Fort Sumter

Our country was torn apart in 1861 by a civil war between the North (Union) and the South (Confederacy). The first battle of the war occurred when Confederate forces demanded that Union soldiers give up their control of Fort Sumter in the harbor at Charleston, South Carolina. Courageously the Union troops refused. They were outnumbered and short on food and ammunition. But they held the fort until Confederate cannons finally opened fire.

Ivy Green, Helen Keller's Home

In 1882 a two-year-old girl in Tuscumbia, Alabama, became very sick and could no longer see or hear. Her world became one of darkness and silence. The child, Helen Keller, gradually overcame her fear and loneliness. Using her sense of touch, she learned to speak again and to read Braille. She graduated from college and went on to inspire others to find courage in their own hearts, just as she had, to overcome their limitations and make the most of their talents.

Vietnam Veterans Memorial

In the 1960s America found itself fighting a war in faraway Vietnam. A quiet voice inside their hearts told some Americans that the war was wrong, and they found the courage to resist the government because of their beliefs. Some went to jail; some left the country. For others the voice of duty called clearly to them to serve their country on battlefields halfway around the world. Some never came back. Their memorial in Washington, D.C., honors the courage that led them to sacrifice for what they believed.

Christa McAuliffe

It takes a special kind of courage to go where no one has gone before. At first astronauts were all trained pilots. Then in 1986, an "ordinary" citizen—a teacher—became part of a mission crew for the first time. From many volunteers the space program selected Christa McAuliffe to serve aboard *Challenger*. Her assignment was to teach a class from space. She never had the chance: *Challenger* exploded on take-off. But Christa McAuliffe's courage still inspires a nation of pioneers.

Hard Work

The life of a pioneer is not an easy one. Americans know that it takes a great deal of effort to build a nation. They understand too that a great nation is also a hard-working one.

Sutter's Mill

America's mining industry boomed in 1848 when gold was discovered near Sutter's Mill in California. Prospectors came running in search of a chance to "get rich quick." Standing for hours in cold mountain streams and sifting through rocks and pebbles for a few flecks of gold, they soon found that mining required endless days of backbreaking labor. Later prospectors also mined the silver, lead, copper, and other minerals that helped make America a rich industrial nation.

Promontory Point

Linking East and West by railroad was a dream that could only be achieved by hard work. Thousands of laborers, many of them recent Irish immigrants, toiled to lay tracks westward across the Great Plains, throwing wooden bridges across rivers and hammering the rails in place. Pushing eastward, Chinese workers scaled lofty mountain peaks, cut tunnels through solid granite, and shoveled away tons of snow. Their goal was reached when these hard-working crews joined their tracks at Promontory Point, Utah, in 1869.

Dodge City

With the opening of the new railroad came boom times for the cattle industry. Ranchers in the Southwest had learned ranching from their Mexican neighbors. Now they could send their herds on the "long drive" to railroad junctions like Dodge City, Kansas. Shipped on by rail, the cattle provided beef for the growing cities of the East. And the cowhands, weary after months of hard labor along the trail, celebrated wildly before turning back to Texas and another long, strenuous drive the following year.

Thomas Edison

He started working in 1859 at age 12, selling newspapers on a train. At 15 he was a telegraph operator, a job he held until he was fired for spending too much time on his inventions. For the rest of his life, Thomas Edison would be an inventor—not through luck, but because he spent so much time in his laboratory. Each invention, from the phonograph to the light bulb to all kinds of electrical equipment, was the result of careful tests and long hours of concentration.

Education for All

Good citizens need good education. Since colonial times, when every town in Massachusetts was required to provide a free public school, America's schools have taught the value of liberty, courage, hard work, and independence.

One-Room Schoolhouse

For many rural and small-town Americans, their first taste of education came in a one-room schoolhouse. Students from kindergarten to eighth grade all learned together, taught by one teacher. Older students helped the younger ones with lessons. Children learned the basics —reading, spelling, writing, and arithmetic— but they also learned the importance of home, family, and country. Angle Inlet School still carries on this tradition, educating children in an isolated part of northern Minnesota.

Oberlin College

Many of our country's early colleges and universities were church schools whose main job was to train preachers. Gradually states began to establish public universities, and colleges offered their students a wider choice of subjects. But until 1833 only men could attend college. That year Oberlin College, a private school in Ohio, admitted female students for the first time. The nation had begun a long journey toward equal educational opportunity for all students.

Tuskegee Institute

Booker T. Washington realized that former slaves like himself could not be truly free until they had a chance to educate themselves. He opened the Tuskegee Institute in Alabama to provide African Americans with a good, practical education. George Washington Carver, one of the school's teachers, helped poor farmers discover the value of crops such as peanuts and sweet potatoes. Together Carver and Washington proved that America grew stronger when all Americans had a chance for an education.

William Holmes McGuffey

Millions of America's children first learned to read from the pages of *McGuffey's Readers*, first published in the 1830s. From these books they learned to recognize letters, sound out words, and appreciate good stories. The stories told of family life and adventures in days gone by. Each story taught a lesson about hard work, charity, courage, patriotism, or respect for parents. With these books children learned not only how to read, but also the ideals their country expected them to live by.

Diversity

American coins all carry the motto *e pluribus unum*, Latin for "one out of many." It means that Americans come from many backgrounds, but we are one people united by the ideals we all share.

St. Augustine

The first Europeans to settle in America were not Pilgrims or Puritans. They were colonists from Spain, and they built America's first European city in St. Augustine, Florida, in 1565. Later other Spaniards settled Santa Fe, New Mexico. In Florida, California, Texas, and the Southwest, new Americans spoke Spanish, not English. The Spanish came first as adventurers, hoping to strike gold and then return home. They soon realized that America offered an ideal place to settle, raise a family, and build a new life.

Williamsburg

English settlers in Virginia had lived in Jamestown for almost a century when they decided that they needed a new capital city for their growing colony. They were still English enough to name the city Williamsburg in honor of their king. But they were also American enough to build a university there, the College of William and Mary, so they could educate their children. And they included a meeting hall for their House of Burgesses, the first assembly to make laws for an American colony.

Chinatown

Chinese immigrants began settling in San Francisco in the 1840s. The Gold Rush brought many more immigrants from China. Some went into the mining camps, while others stayed to open stores and businesses in the city. Thousands more arrived in the 1860s to build the Central Pacific Railroad. San Francisco soon became home to the largest community of Chinese anywhere in the world outside of China itself. Here Chinese Americans honor both American ideals and Chinese traditions.

Code Talkers

Our diversity proved valuable during World War II. When the Marines needed a code for radio communications, they turned to Native American recruits who spoke Navajo. Only a few non-Navajo people spoke the language, so enemy forces could not understand the messages these "code talkers" broadcast. The code talkers' skill, speed, and accuracy contributed to every American victory in the South Pacific.

Free Enterprise

America is a nation built on independent businesses, whether they are family farms, small offices, or large factories. Behind every successful business is an entrepreneur—someone with a good idea and the willingness to work hard.

Slater's Mill

America owes much of its industrial strength to a young immigrant, Samuel Slater. A mill worker in England, Slater convinced several wealthy investors to pay for the building of America's first real factory in Pawtucket, Rhode Island. Instead of using skilled artisans to make things, Slater's innovative system used machinery that could be run by unskilled laborers. Workers, many of them immigrants, found jobs here and helped turn America into a great industrial nation.

River Rouge

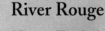

Henry Ford also built his cars on a factory system, but he added a new idea. In his plant near Detroit, the car being built moved along an assembly line. Each worker did just one simple job, adding one more piece to the vehicle. At the end of the line, the completed car rolled off and was driven away. Ford paid good wages so that his workers—and others like them—could afford to buy his cars. By producing quality at a low price, he turned a luxury item into something that almost every American could own.

Magic Kingdom

Only in America could a cartoon mouse turn into an entertainment industry. Walt Disney caught the imagination of moviegoers with cartoons featuring Mickey Mouse, and later, with full-length animated films. He realized that Americans were looking for places where whole families could enjoy vacationing together. Like all good entrepreneurs, he understood what people wanted. At Magic Kingdom in Florida, one of his theme parks, people of all ages can enjoy fantasy, adventure, and excitement.

Madame C. J. Walker

Inventiveness is a characteristic of most entrepreneurs. Madame C. J. Walker developed a line of hair care and beauty products that she manufactured in her home and sold door-to-door. She was so successful that within a few years she opened her own factory and built a sales force of 20,000 people. One of America's first female millionaires, she often told people, "If I have been able to accomplish anything it is because I have been willing to work hard."

25

Creative Spirit

One of the freedoms our Constitution protects is the right to express our ideas as we see fit. Over the years, Americans have exercised this right and shared their ideas in many creative ways—through speeches, writing, music, art, and dance.

Preservation Hall

Even under slavery, the human spirit found ways to express itself. African Americans developed a rich tradition of spirituals and created the slow, haunting melodies that we call "the blues." And they invented the rhythms and harmony of jazz. Jazz musicians love improvisation—each instrument "doing its own thing," yet still blending perfectly with the other instruments. Every night at Preservation Hall in New Orleans, jazz fans gather to enjoy this African American contribution to American cultural life.

St. James Theater

America was at war in the spring of 1943 when a new play opened on Broadway in New York. It was the earliest example of another unique American contribution to the arts, the musical comedy. Musical comedy is words, music, and dance working together to tell a story. This first real musical comedy, *Oklahoma!*, was special, too, because it was a story of America's past and reminded Americans what they were fighting for.

Hollywood

Since the early 1900s, Hollywood, California, has been home to the actors, writers, directors, costume designers, lighting technicians, makeup artists, and sound engineers who produce movies that entertain America and the world. The word "Hollywood" today means more than just a section of Los Angeles. It stands for all the adventure, romance, comedy, and drama of the movies. The artists of Hollywood bring us together through the magic of their films.

Marian Anderson

One of the most beautiful voices ever heard in America belonged to Marian Anderson. She often faced discrimination because she was African American. For one concert in Washington, D.C., in 1939, she was told she could not sing where she had planned. She arranged instead to sing at the Lincoln Memorial to a crowd of 75,000 people. In that concert her pure, sweet voice showed all Americans that talent and creativity are shared, and are meant to be enjoyed, by all races equally.

Honor

"Duty, honor, country"—these three words form the motto of the United States Military Academy at West Point. They are words and ideals that have inspired not only soldiers, but also ordinary citizens throughout our country's history.

Appomattox Court House

On April 9, 1865, General Robert E. Lee surrendered to General Ulysses S. Grant at the McLean farmhouse in Appomattox Court House, Virginia. Both men had led their armies through the terrible four-year Civil War. Both men believed they were doing their duty and serving their country. At the end, each man treated the other with honor. In their own way, these two great leaders helped the country understand that the war was over and the nation was one again.

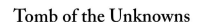

Tomb of the Unknowns

There are times when our nation has had to fight to preserve the ideals we all believe in. In those awful times of war, men and women soldiers know that they may be asked to give their lives in defense of their country. Many of our brave dead are unidentified. In memory of all these nameless heroes, our nation dedicated the Tomb of the Unknowns at Arlington National Cemetery in Arlington, Virginia. They served their country with honor and helped keep the flame of liberty alive.

New York City Firehouse

Every day across America, our nation's police officers and firefighters face unknown dangers as they serve and protect the public. Their duty takes them into dark streets and burning buildings. With courage they face danger to protect the lives of others. Every year some lose their lives in the line of duty. At the Engine 54, Ladder 4 Firehouse in New York City, flowers pay tribute to a group of heroes who served and died with honor in the terrible tragedy of September 11, 2001.

Nathan Hale

During the Revolutionary War, a young Connecticut schoolteacher named Nathan Hale followed the call of duty and joined General Washington's army in New York. His mission was to discover information about where the British troops would attack next. Captured by British troops, Hale was brought to trial and convicted of spying. The penalty was death by hanging. As he was led to the gallows, a British officer reported that Hale's last words were, "I regret that I have but one life to lose for my country."

When and Where

Unless otherwise noted, dates listed for places indicate founding or the beginning of construction.
Dates listed for people are life spans.

8000 B.C.: Acoma Pueblo, NM

1565: St. Augustine, FL

1607: Jamestown, VA

1620: Plymouth Rock, Plymouth, MA

1699: Williamsburg, VA

1743–1826: Thomas Jefferson

1755–1776: Nathan Hale

1775: Revolutionary War begins at Concord Bridge, Concord, MA

1776: Declaration of Independence signed at Independence Hall, Philadelphia, PA

1777: Valley Forge, VA

ca. 1786–1812: Sacagawea

1789: Bill of Rights adopted at Federal Hall, New York, NY

1793: The Capitol, Washington, DC

1793: Slater's Mill, Pawtucket, RI

1800–1873: William Holmes McGuffey

1800: The White House, Washington, DC

1812: USS *Constitution*'s greatest battles; now docked in Boston, MA

1821–1912: Clara Barton

1833: Women admitted to Oberlin College, Oberlin, OH

1839: Levi Coffin House, Fountain City, IN

1840s: Great Migration of settlers from Scotts Bluff, NE

1846: Chinatown, San Francisco, CA

1847–1931: Thomas Edison

1848: Women's Rights Convention at Wesleyan Chapel, Seneca Falls, NY

1848: Sutter's Mill, Coloma, CA

1850s: One-Room Schoolhouse, Angle Inlet, MN

1861: Civil War begins at Fort Sumter, SC

1862: Homestead Act passed; memorialized at Homestead National Monument, Beatrice, NE

1865: Civil War ends in Appomattox Court House, VA

1867–1919: Madame C. J. Walker

1869: Railroads meet at Promontory Point, UT

1872: Dodge City, KS

1880: Tuskegee Institute, Tuskegee, AL

1882: Helen Keller falls ill at Ivy Green, Tuscumbia, AL

1897–1993: Marian Anderson

1890s–1920s: Jazz flourishes at Preservation Hall, New Orleans, LA

1908–1993: Thurgood Marshall

1910s–1920s: Studios expand in Hollywood, CA

1921: Tomb of the Unknowns, Arlington, VA

1927: River Rouge, Dearborn, MI

1927–1993: Cesar Chavez

1929–1968: Martin Luther King Jr.

Sutter's Mill, Coloma, CA

Chinatown, San Francisco, CA

Manzanar, Independence, CA

Hollywood, CA

1935: The Supreme Court, Washington, DC

1941–1945: World War II; Marines use code talkers

1942: Manzanar, Independence, CA

1943: *Oklahoma!* opens at the St. James Theater, New York, NY

1948–1986: Christa McAuliffe

1960: First election as "first in the nation" for Dixville Notch, NH

1962: Kennedy Space Center, Cape Canaveral, FL

1971: Magic Kingdom, Orlando, FL

1982: Vietnam Veterans Memorial, Washington, DC

2001: Terrorist attacks; memorials at Engine 54, Ladder 4 Firehouse, New York, NY

Homestead National
Monument, Beatrice, NE

Levi Coffin House,
Fountain City, IN

omontory Point, UT

Scotts Bluff, NE

One-Room Schoolhouse
Angle Inlet, MN

River Rouge, Dearborn, MI

Dixville Notch, NH

Oberlin
College, OH

Wesleyan Chapel
Seneca Falls, NY

Concord Bridge, MA
USS *Constitution*, Boston, MA
Plymouth Rock, MA

Slater's Mill, Pawtucket, RI

New York City, NY
Federal Hall Memorial
St. James Theater
NYC Firehouse

Valley Forge, PA
Independence Hall, Philadelphia, PA

Washington, DC
The Capitol
The White House
The Supreme Court
Vietnam Veterans Memorial

Tomb of the Unknowns, Arlington, VA
Williamsburg, VA
Jamestown, VA
Appomattox Court House, VA

Ft. Sumter, SC

St. Augustine, FL

Magic Kingdom,
Orlando, FL

Kennedy Space Center,
Cape Canaveral, FL

Acoma Pueblo, NM

Dodge City, KS

Preservation Hall,
New Orleans, LA

Tuskeegee
Institute, AL

Ivy Green, Tuscumbia, AL

31

Resources

Liberty

Giblin, James Cross, illustrated by Michael Dooling. *Thomas Jefferson: A Picture Book Biography.* New York: Scholastic, 1994.

Peacock, Judith. *The Battles of Lexington and Concord.* Mankato, MN: Bridgestone Books, 2002.

USS *Constitution*: http://www.ussconstitution.navy.mil

Equality

Fritz, Jean, illustrated by DyAnne DiSalvo-Ryan. *You Want Women to Vote, Lizzie Stanton?* New York: Putnam, 1995.

Hansen, Joyce, and Gary McGowan, illustrated by James Ransome. *Freedom Roads: Searching for the Underground Railroad.* Chicago: Cricket Books, 2003.

Patent, Dorothy Hinshaw. *Homesteading: Settling America's Heartland.* New York: Walker & Company, 1998.

Rappaport, Doreen, illustrated by Bryan Collier. *Martin's Big Words: The Life of Dr. Martin Luther King, Jr.* New York: Jump at the Sun/ Hyperion, 2001.

Legal Rights

Krull, Kathleen, illustrated by Yuri Morales. *Harvesting Hope: The Story of Cesar Chavez.* New York: Harcourt, 2003.

Plimoth Plantation. *Mayflower 1620: A New Look at a Pilgrim Voyage.* Washington, D.C.: National Geographic Society, 2003.

Steen, Sandra, and Susan Steen. *Independence Hall.* New York: Dillon Press, 1994.

Rule of Law

Adler, David A., illustrated by Robert Casilla. *A Picture Book of Thurgood Marshall.* New York: Holiday House, 1997.

Binns, Tristan Boyer. *The White House.* Chicago: Heinemann, 2001.

Britton, Tamara L. *The Capitol.* Edina, MN: ABDO Publishing, 2003.

LeVert, Suzanne. *The Supreme Court.* Tarrytown, NY: Benchmark Books, 2003.

Pioneer Spirit

Erdrich, Lise, illustrated by Julie Buffalohead. *Sacagawea.* Minneapolis: Carolrhoda Books, 2003.

Pueblo of Acoma—Sky City: http://www.puebloofacoma.org

Spangenburg, Ray, and Kit Moser. *The History of NASA.* New York: Franklin Watts, 2000.

Wadsworth, Ginger. *Words West: Voices of Young Pioneers.* New York: Clarion, 2003.

Hardship

Bunting, Eve, illustrated by Chris Soenpiet. *So Far From the Sea.* New York: Clarion, 1998.

Francis, Dorothy Brenner. *Clara Barton: Founder of the American Red Cross.* Brookfield, CT: Millbrook, 2002.

Sewall, Marcia. *James Towne: Struggle for Survival.* New York: Atheneum, 2001.

Stein, R. Conrad. *Valley Forge.* Chicago: Children's Press, 1994.

Courage

Adler, David A., illustrated by John Wallner. *A Picture Book of Helen Keller.* New York: Holiday House, 2003.

Ashabranner, Brent, photos by Jennifer Ashabranner. *Their Names to Live: What the Vietnam Veterans Memorial Means to America.* New York: Twenty-First Century Books, 1998.

Haskins, Jim. *The Day Fort Sumter Was Fired On: A Photo History of the Civil War.* New York: Scholastic, 1995.

Streissguth, Thomas. *Christa McAuliffe.* Mankato, MN: Bridgestone Books, 2003.

Hard Work

Delano, Marfe Ferguson. *Inventing the Future: A Photobiography of Thomas Alva Edison.* Washington, DC: National Geographic, 2002.

Dolan, Edward F. *The Transcontinental Railroad.* New York: Benchmark Books/Marshall Cavendish, 2003.

Engstrand, Iris, and Kenneth N. Owens. *John Sutter: Sutter's Fort and the California Gold Rush.* New York: PowerKids Press, 2004.

Stanley, Jerry. *Cowboys and Longhorns: A Portrait of the Long Drive.* New York: Crown, 2003.

Education for All

Edwards, Linda McMurry. *George Washington Carver: The Life of the Great American Agriculturist.* New York: PowerKids Press, 2004.

Graves, Kerry A. *Going to School in Pioneer Times.* Mankato, MN: Capstone Press, 2002.

McKissack, Patricia and Fred. *The Story of Booker T. Washington.* Chicago: Children's Press, 1991.

Diversity

Aaseng, Nathan. *Navajo Code Talkers: America's Secret Weapon in World War II.* New York: Walker, 1992.

Brenner, Barbara. *If You Lived in Williamsburg in Colonial Days.* New York: Scholastic, 2000.

Isaacs, Sally Senzel. *Life in St. Augustine.* Chicago: Heinemann, 2003.

Isaacs, Sally Senzel. *Life in San Francisco's Chinatown.* Chicago: Heinemann, 2003.

Free Enterprise

Bagley, Katie. *The Early American Industrial Revolution 1793-1850.* Mankato, MN: Capstone Press, 2003.

Ford, Carin T. *Walt Disney: Meet the Cartoonist.* Berkeley Heights, NJ: Enslow, 2003.

Gourley, Catherine. *Wheels of Time: A Biography of Henry Ford.* Brookfield, CT: Millbrook, 1997.

Lasky, Kathryn, illustrated by Nneka Bennett. *Vision of Beauty: The Story of Sarah Breedlove Walker.* Cambridge, MA: Candlewick, 2000.

Creative Spirit

Asirvathan, Sandy. *The History of Jazz.* Philadelphia: Chelsea House, 2003.

Film History of the 1920s: http://www.filmsite.org/20sintro.html

Ryan, Pam Muñoz, illustrated by Brian Selznick. *When Marian Sang: The True Recital of Marian Anderson.* New York: Scholastic, 2002.

Honor

Houghton, Gillian. *Grant and Lee at Appomattox: A Primary Source History of the End of the Civil War.* New York: Rosen, 2003.

Kritzner, L. J. and Lisa Sita. *Nathan Hale: Patriot and Martyr of the American Revolution.* New York: Rosen, 2002.

Stein, R. Conrad. *Arlington National Cemetery.* Chicago: Children's Press, 1995.